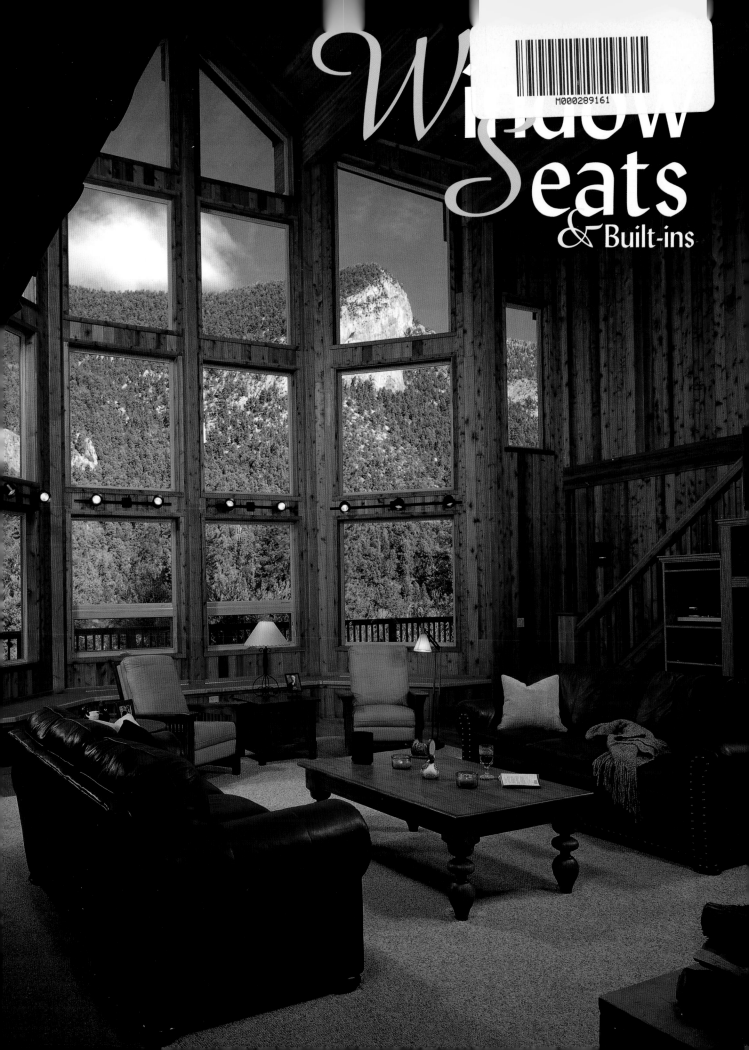

# Window Seats
## & Built-ins

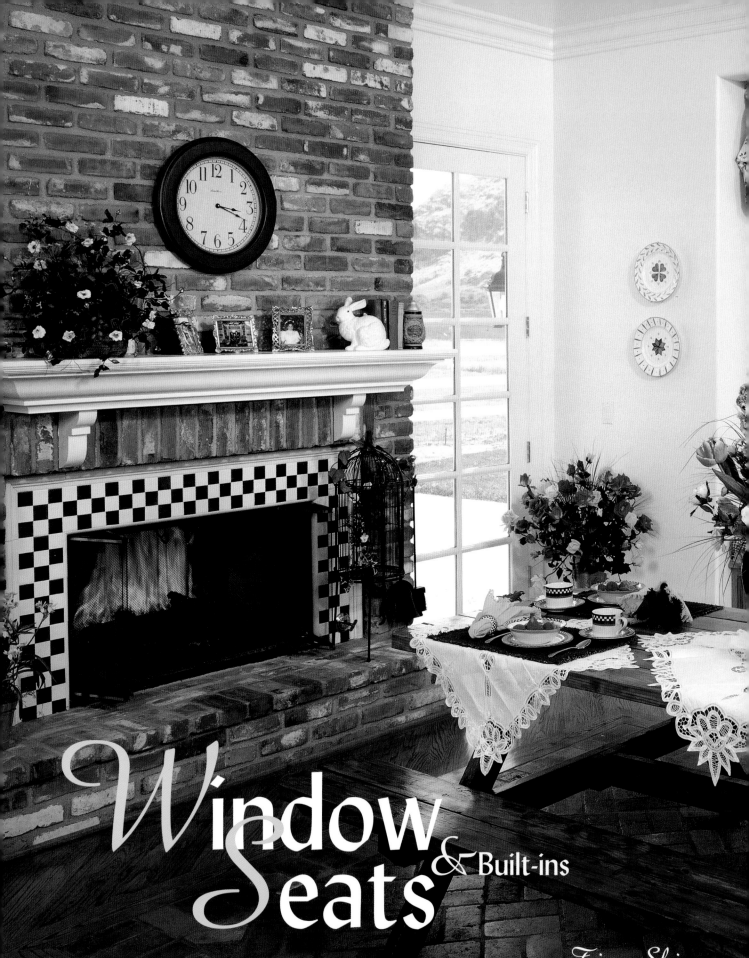

# Window
# Seats
## & Built-ins

### Tina Skinner

Schiffer
Publishing Ltd

4880 Lower Valley Road, Atglen, PA 19310 USA

Library of Congress  Cataloging-in-Publication Data
Skinner, Tina.
Window seats & built-ins / by Tina Skinner.
p. cm.
ISBN 0-7643-1933-7 (pbk.)
1. Built-in-furniture--Pictorial works. 2. Interior decoration. I. Title: Window seats and built-ins.
II. Title.
TT197.5.B8 S57 2004
684.1'6--dc21
2003009358

Published by Schiffer Publishing Ltd.
4880 Lower Valley Road
Atglen, PA 19310
Phone: (610) 593-1777; Fax: (610) 593-2002
E-mail: Info@schifferbooks.com
Please visit our web site catalog at **www.schifferbooks.com**
We are always looking for people to write books on new and related subjects. If you have an idea for a book, please contact us at the above address.

This book may be purchased from the publisher. Include $3.95 for shipping. Please try your bookstore first. You may write for a free catalog.

In Europe, Schiffer books are distributed by
Bushwood Books
6 Marksbury Avenue
Kew Gardens
Surrey TW9 4JF England
Phone: 44 (0) 20 8392 8585; Fax: 44 (0) 20 8392 9876
E-mail: Bushwd@aol.com
Free postage in the UK. Europe: air mail at cost.

Designed by Bonnie M. Hensley - Cover design by Bruce Waters
Type set in Amazone BT/Lydian BT/Zurich LtCn BT

ISBN: 0-7643-1933-7
Printed in China

# Acknowledgments

A coworker's reaction to the news that I was working on a window seat book was typical. Her story went like this:

"I used to have a window seat when I was a little girl. It had a little cubby underneath where I kept toys, and I spent hours sitting there playing. A lot of my childhood memories take place in that window seat."

I myself have a favorite college memory, actually, of curling up in a stairwell window overlooking the University of Delaware mall. There, in the quiet Memorial Hall, I'd escape into a book (studying literature is such a great excuse for getting educated!). I felt washed by the sunshine outside, sequestered and relaxed.

Ever since I began obsessing with the idea of a window seat book, I've been seeing them everywhere, in particular on children's television programs. My casual observations of my daughter's favorite shows have led me to the conclusion that set designers include window seats in two out of three children's sets. Why not? Given the opportunity to create an idyllic space, who wouldn't toss a comfy seat under the window.

When you think about it, we spend most of our time in the house sitting, whereas most windows only work view-wise when you stand. So adding a window seat and snuggling up to the view only makes sense.

This book was kept short and sweet, with an eye toward inspiring architects, designers, and homeowners in the many opportunities to furnish a window, and to decorate it to make it an inviting mini room in and of itself. Treated properly, a window becomes the captain's seat in a porthole between the indoors and out. Seated here, the occupant is master of both worlds, connected to both, and in a position of semi-isolation betwixt the two.

Adding a couch or comfy chair eats up little more space than the walls. Because window seats are such space savers, this book also encompasses a few examples of built-in seating. Incredible space can be added, along with comfort, with basic built-ins.

As a result of this book, I've finally managed to design my own window seat. Lacking a bay window, or a small nook somewhere perfect for placing a built-in, I purchased four handsome toy boxes and cobbled them together under a long wall of windows, adding padding and pillows. Now I've got one of the most popular hangouts in the house. It draws people away from the couch and the dining chairs only a couple of feet away in either direction, and invites them to perch closest to the view of the woods behind our home.

My daughter, now three, is already capitalizing on the added space. The boxes have become her secret stash places, and she's often opening them to reveal her hidden treasures. Sometimes this is to our great dismay, as in the case of unwrapped chocolate candies, or mom's missing watch. Sometimes the source of great amusement, as in the treasured packaging for a doll she received from Santa.

I wish you well in creating a window seat for your home, and in the memories you and your children will build there.

8

Courtesy of Wood-Mode/Design by Jane Victor

This decorative mud room, complete with custom cabinetry, provides space for an equestrian to sit and pull on those knee-high boots.

Two walls of windows overlook the ocean, and a window seat takes maximum advantage of the view.

This comfy bench is a good place to stop and rest upon arriving home after being out and about all day. Nearby hooks provide a home for jackets, purses, and other personal items.

A bench is a critical component in custom cabinetry that serves
as coat rack and storage for all the children's school items.

Pillows and a cushion offer the perfect place to meditate beneath a cathedral ceiling.

13

Commanding a bay window, a deep bench seat overlooks the courtyard area.

Courtesy of Wood-Mode/Design by Sue Patterson

16

Comfy red cushions underline a great sweep of windowpanes.

*Opposite page:*
Handsome redwood trims a bow window and creates a
broad perch where one can soak in the view.

A wall of windows is underlined by
a colorful V of seating.

19

A mountain view is unfettered by unnecessary ornament, simply framed in rich wood.

Swimmers can get a first glance at the inviting pool beyond, while towels and other swimming essentials can be stored in the surrounding cabinets.

A private corner in a family room, the window seat offers a place to get away
from the television, yet be close to the viewers.

A window seat crowns a bookshelf in this cozy living room.

A new window and wall
cabinets include a seat,
because with a corner like this,
who wouldn't want to sit in it?

24

Pretty blue accents
highlight a crisp blue room.

26

A blend of silk and velvet give this romantic
window seat a delicate, feminine touch.

Courtesy of Gracious Living Interiors/Design by Melinda Kuehne/Photo by Randy Bye

Cherishing their open floor space, the owners have pushed seating back against windows and walls.

A bear family has moved in to occupy one window seat, and plants soak up the sun in another.

*Top left:* Two walls of bookcases and cabinetry include a soft window seat in this home library.

*Top right:* Handsome curtains add shape to a pair of window seats that flank fireplace and an entertainment center.

*Bottom left:* Comfy cushions and warm sunlight make this window seat a great place for a catnap.

*Bottom right:* This Prairie-style wooden cabinet provides the perfect opportunity to turn an otherwise plain radiator into a beautiful window seat.

A cushion caps built-in storage and bookcases, and offers a quick resting spot in a spare bedroom located in reclaimed attic space.

A good book and a hot cup of coffee or tea are the only things missing from this cozy, sunny window seat. Built-in drawers below offer attractive storage.

A window seat provides both visual and physical comfort. The colors of
sunshine and spring make it even more inviting.

Textiles create exotic allure in a window retreat.

31

A cornered end offers a solution for a window seat with only one wall to butt up against.

Courtesy of Charles Cabinet Co.

An exterior staircase presents unique architectural opportunities within.

Courtesy of Glidden

Courtesy of Charles Cabinet Co.

Vented woodwork artfully disguises a heating unit that doubles as super cozy seating in wintertime.

Cabinetry above and below added much-needed storage to a kitchen, while sacrificing little space.

33

Courtesy of Charles Cabinet Co.

A semi-circle of seating in a bow window makes for a memorable eat-in kitchen.

A window seat offers a perch in a work-oriented kitchen, keeping visitors out from underfoot.

Courtesy of KraftMaid Cabinetry

Courtesy of Simonton Windows

*Left:* Columns support a ceiling in a large, open room. Tucked below is semi-private seating where one can help out, or simply taste the cook's best efforts.

*Right:* Bow windows are created by mulling together three or more windows at 30- or 45-degree angles.

36

*Opposite page:*
Textiles used on the dining seat covers are repeated in accent pillows for the window seat.

37

Courtesy of Anthony Totilo Architects, Darien, CT & Olson Photographic, LLC

Whimsical splashes of color and wood carved wood elements add to this arcing kitchen arrangement, complete with built-in seating backed by a buffet counter.

45

A bench is an easy alternative to built-in.

Bench seating is upholstered in blues and earth
tones, tying in to the blue tiling and wine rack and
the rich wood finish on the cabinetry.

Courtesy of Bis Bis Imports Boston

Courtesy of Wood-Mode/Design by Lorena Oden

By placing seating against a wall, a room is expanded. In this case, company can hang out in the kitchen without getting in the way.

Courtesy of Wood-Mode/Design by Norman Rosner

Tucked into an ell off the kitchen, a private little seat offers a window for peaking and a countertop for a teacup or a small project.

*Left:* Faux animal skins add drama.

*Right:* Built into a corner, bench seating simultaneously offers a view and a seat at the table.

*Left:* Bright accent colors heighten a room's appeal.

*Right:* A little retreat at the top of the stairs is the perfect place to slip away with a spot of tea while watching for the arrival of someone special.

A breakfast nook area seems larger with bench seating, and room was reserved for accessing storage and display cabinets.

Courtesy of Wood-Mode/Design by John A. Buscarello, ASID

A bench seat offers a place to take off your shoes upon entering the
back door, in an alcove leading to a walk-through kitchen.

49

50

A small window seat offers repose at the foot of the family stairs, just before one enters an open kitchen area.

52

Seating is offered fireside for diners, or one might take advantage of the room during non-dining hours for a private retreat.

54

Giving up cabinets for a wall of light hardly seems a sacrifice for this kitchen.

Adorned with colorful, decorative pillows and cushions, and providing convenient storage, this wall-length bench also adds informal seating for additional guests.

A built-in breakfast nook becomes a family getaway for three-squares a day.

*Left:* The padded bench is the preferred seating when all family members are present.

*Right:* A beautiful window works like a magnet.

59

The little architectural folly between two storage areas creates a focal point, and allows for a cozy little window seat with an optional shuttered view.

In modifying a large room, designer Cheryl Casey Ross wanted to add charm, and she needed to provide seating for large family gatherings. Fabrics were important to baffle the openness of the space, so pillows and curtains were lavished on the seat.

Courtesy of Charles Cabinet Co.

A shelf area below a picture window can be used for seating or display.

Courtesy of Cross Interiors/Photography by Mark Lohman

Courtesy of Wood-Mode/Design by Bonni Armstrong and Pam Fink

Built-in cabinetry and a wall-long window seat add space to a contemporary addition.

Built-in storage and shelves make way for a fantastic view, with front-row seating.

A custom window invites one in for a porthole peak at the deck beyond.

Courtesy of Harrison Design Associates

Today's master bedroom suites often include room for a sofa and two chairs. This remodel didn't allow for that much space, but a window seat is a happy substitute.

Green trim lends a summer cottage feel to this guest room.

70

A quilt and pillows make this spacious ledge a place where one can curl up for a cat-like nap in the sun.

Courtesy of Gregory Interiors, LLC, Essex, CT & Olson Photographic, LLC

Red and white fabrics and wall treatments work together for a decidedly feminine retreat.

A window seat offers room for a second adult to ogle the infant in this charming nursery.

Feminine white textiles soften handsome woodwork.

A sweet little seat is a leg-swinging spot for a wee one when mom is pampering herself in this wonderful walk-in closet.

A window seat hugs a V-shaped window arrangement in a room
rife with architectural interest.

This comfy stretch of window is where
a princess's pastel-shaded memories
will be made.

Courtesy of Glidden

A playroom is perfect in pink, made complete with a window seat that takes advantage of the attic window.

After-school sports can be tiresome, and here an active young athlete can rest up before tackling their homework.

Courtesy of Georgia-Pacific

Siblings share a view in a room replete with custom niceties – hand painted
furniture, custom throw pillows, and other charming bits of farm art.

A lazy soak in this therapeutic whirlpool tub is almost as appealing as a tranquil gaze to the outdoors from the sun-splashed window seat.

If you want someone to wash your back, it helps to provide a seat.

79

Shades draw up or down to allow bathers a choice of privacy or view.

Proportionate to the window, and mimicking it in form, an oval tub sits within a classic surround by the mullioned view.

A tile surround offers a dry ledge encircling
a spacious whirlpool tub.

Porthole-size windows offer private peaks at the
outdoors, while leaving the bather a sense of privacy.

Set within a luxurious tile surround, a bathroom bench invites two to linger and discuss the upcoming day.

Here's a great seat, sans view. Built into a spacious shower, a tiled bench offers an opportunity to groom your toenails or fuss between shampoos.

Originally the master bath, a young girl benefited from the remodel. A window seat was a must, allowing her a place to sit with friends when they visited and, when not in use, as a place to display her animal and doll collection along with coordinating pillows.

Strips and paisley upholster an inviting expanse of window seat.

A cushiony window seat offers a place of repose in this home office.

A small ledge allows a family member to drop by this home office, but not to get too comfy.

Narrow bookcases border a built-in seat and drawer.

Matching woodwork frames windows, wall, and seat.

A simple chaise lounge fulfills the need for relaxing in the sun.

A lounge chair fills in for seating beneath a dramatic arch of panes.

# Resource Guide

Bis Bis Imports Boston
4 Park Plaza
Boston, MA 02116
617-350-7565
www.bisbis.com

California Closets
1000 Fourth Street, Suite 800
San Rafael, CA 94901
800-274-6754
www.calclosets.com

California Redwood Association
405 Enfrente Drive, Suite 200
Novato, CA 94949
415-382-0662
www.calredwood.org

Charles Cabinet Co.
3090 N. Cleveland avenue
Roseville, MN 55113
651-633-1488
www.charlescabinetco.com

Congoleum Corp.
3500 Quakerbridge Road
Mercerville, NJ 08619-0127
800-274-3266
www.congoleum.com

Cross Interiors
6712 Colbath Avenue
Van Nuys, CA 91405
818-988-2047
www.crossinteriors.com

Crossville Porcelain Stone/USA
P.O. Box 1168
Crossville, TN 38557
931-484-2110
www.crossville-ceramics.com

Decorá
One MasterBrand Cabinets Drive
Jasper, IN 47546
812-482-2527
www.mbcabinets.com

Embellishments
Interior Designs by Lea Anne
11 Albany Street
Cazenovia, NY 13035
315-655-8265
interiorsbylea-anne.com

Georgia-Pacific
P.O. Box 740075
Atlanta, GA 30374-0075
1-800-BUILD-GP
www.georgia-pacific.com

The Glidden Company
925 Euclid Avenue
Cleveland, OH 44115
800-GLIDDEN
www.gliddenpaint.com

Gracious Living Home
Rt 202
Lahaska, PA
215-794-4118

Gracious Living Interiors
370 W. Bridge Street
New Hope, PA
215-862-3304
www.graciousinteriors.com

Harrison Design Associates
3198 Cains Hill Place, NW Suite 200
Atlanta, GA 30305
404-365-7760
www.Harrisondesignassociates.com

Jim Bishop Cabinets, Inc.
P.O. Box 11424
Montgomery, AL 36111
800-410-2444, ext. 3017
www.jimbishopcabinets.com

Kohler Co.
444 Highland Drive
Kohler, WI 53044
1-800-4-KOHLER
www.kohler.com

KraftMaid Cabinetry
PO Box 1055
Middlefield, OH 44062
800-571-1990
www.kraftmaid.com

Kemper Distinctive Cabinetry
One MasterBrand Cabinets Drive
Jasper, IN 47546
812-482-2527
www.mbcabinets.com

Lindal Cedar Homes
4300 South 104th Place
Seattle, WA 98178
206-725-0900
www.lindal.com

Olson Photographic, LLC
37 Shore Drive
Higganum, CT 06441
860-345-3744
www.olsonphotographic.com

Peter Cadoux Architects, P.C.
44 Post Road West
Westport, CT
203-227-4304
www.cadouxaia.com

Plain & Fancy Custom Cabinetry
Route 501 & Oak Street
P.O. Box 519
Schaefferstown, PA 17088
800-447-9006
www.plainfancycabinetry.com

Simonton Windows
5300 Briscoe Road
Parkersburg, WV 26102
(800) SIMONTON
www.simonton.com

Sroka Design, Inc.
7307 Macarthur Blvd., Suite 214
Bethesda, MD 20816
301-263-9100
www.srokadesign.com

Wood-Mode Fine Custom Cabinetry
One Second Street
Kreamer, PA 17833
570-374-2711
www.wood-mode.com

The Wooden Radiator Cabinet Company
P.O. Box 148037
Chicago, IL 60614
800-817-9110
www.woodenradiatorcabinet.com

Yankee Barn Homes
131 Yankee Barn Road
Grantham, NH 03753
603-863-4545
www.yankeebarnhomes.com

MORE SCHIFFER TITLES

**Beautiful Bedrooms, Design Inspirations from the World's Leading Inns and Hotels.** *Tina Skinner*
Enter more than 250 gorgeous guestrooms and get inspiration for your own sleeping quarters. From lofty hideaways to enormous, two-room master suites, you'll find ideas for linens, curtains and upholstery, wallpaper and window seats, beds from four-posters to handcrafted antiques, and whirlpools and fireplaces in the sleeping chamber.
Size: 8 1/2" x 11"     271 color photos     160 pp.
Resource Guide
ISBN: 0-7643-1461-0     hard cover     $29.95

**Beautiful Bathrooms.** *Tina Skinner*
These designer rooms will help you choose your color palette in a style that suits you. A resource guide at the back of the book will help you locate designers and manufacturers who can help mesh your style with the walls and dimensions your home offers.
Size: 8 1/2" x 11"     200 color photos     144 pp.
Resource Guide
ISBN: 0-7643-1536-6     soft cover     $24.95

**Fire Spaces, Design Inspirations for Fireplaces and Stoves.** *Tina Skinner*
Shown within room settings, more than 400 images help you to envision a fireplace as part of your overall decor. Plus, there's an enormous gallery of close-up images showing fireplace and stove details. You'll have trouble choosing just one!
Size: 8 1/2" x 11"     417 color photos     176 pp.
Resource Guide
ISBN: 0-7643-1694-X     hard cover     $34.95

**Great Kitchen Designs, A Visual Feast of Ideas and Resources.** *Tina Skinner*
370 full-color pictures of hundreds of beautiful kitchens to help you create your own unique cooking/dining/entertaining environment. All the elements of beautiful kitchens—flooring, cabinetry, windows, walls, lighting, appliances, surrounds, backsplashes and more—are pictured and discussed. Includes a special chapter on the small kitchen, plus a resource guide listing designers and manufacturers. An invaluable resource for anyone planning to remodel an old kitchen or build a new one and a great reference book for kitchen design professionals.
Size: 8 1/2" x 11"     370 color photos     176 pp.
ISBN: 0-7643-1211-1     soft cover     $29.95

**Barn-Style Homes, Design Ideas for Timber Frame Houses.** *Tina Skinner and Tony Hanslin*
A must-have for anyone who owns or wants to build a timber-frame house, or remodel a barn. Includes stunning images from 37 custom-built homes complete with floor plans. Furnishing and decorating ideas for great rooms, master bedrooms, cozy sitting rooms, elegant dining rooms, home offices, kitchens and baths, and lofty hideaways.
Size: 8 1/2" x 11"     275 color photos, 37 illus     192 pp.
Resource Guide
ISBN: 0-7643-1319-3     hard cover     $39.95

**Creative Patios.** *Tina Skinner*
This collection of beautiful photographs will help you choose a patio style suitable for your home, speak your contractor's language, furnish and organize outdoor areas, create containers and border areas for dynamic gardens and landscaping displays, and develop outdoor sanctuaries with artfully placed planter boxes, shrubs, and privacy screens. Includes step-by-step instructions for installing a paver patio.
Size: 8 1/2" x 11"     310 photos     192 pp.
Resource Guide
ISBN: 0-7643- 1278-2     soft cover     $29.95

**All Decked Out...Redwood Decks, Ideas and Plans for Contemporary Outdoor Living.** *Tina Skinner*
Over 200 color photographs of decks from around the country are presented with plans and ideas for overcoming slopes, incorporating trees, encircling spas, creating conversation pits, and enhancing gardens. Additions like stylized railings or varied floor patterns can suggest Japanese gardens or colonial elegance. A cut-out planner and hints to get started will help refocus life in the great outdoors.
Size: 8 1/2" x 11"     212 color photos/31 illus.     160 pp.
ISBN: 0-7643-0510-7     soft cover     $29.95

**Bright Ideas, Sunrooms & Conservatories.** *Tina Skinner*
Interior and exterior photographs of sunrooms, conservatories, greenhouses, and great glass walls will help you select the right style for your architecture, as well as your lifestyle. Includes ideas for furnishing your indoor extension into the great outdoors, from formal dining areas to comfy family gathering spots, plus tub and pool rooms, patio rooms and indoor gardens, even kitchens and fanciful Florida rooms.
Size: 8 1/2" x 11"     189 photos     160 pp.
Resource Guide
ISBN: 0-7643-1418-1     soft cover     $29.95